threads of light, sewn together

Toby Gui

BookLeaf Publishing

India | USA | UK

Presentation by *BookLeaf Publishing*

Web: www.bookleafpub.com

E-mail: info@bookleafpub.com

ISBN: 9789363308312

First edition 2024

ACKNOWLEDGEMENT

thank you to everyone who has shown me i can
be loved at my most rotted core

introduction to the show

a portfolio to sum up my life, when i've only
lived 16 years of it is daunting. i'm not sure the
best way to go about it, but i don't think it's right
to start this with a litany of tragedies. there is so
much that goes into a single experience, let
alone over a decade's worth of living that i could
not possibly sum up in one work no matter how
lengthy. it does not do me justice to focus on
what has made up my life, stuffy rooms and
quiet nights hunched under the crevice in a
cellar's corner, not when there is so much to
love. i am a collage of everyone who has ever
met me, every work of media and thing
(beautiful or not) i have ever come across. i
think that's something worth noting, worth
being. to love in any regard is to let open the
opportunity to change, leave a part of you to
dwell in them and change for the better.

if you can find it in you, please forgive your
author for his inability to concisely sum up his
beliefs.

what does home mean to you? (a personal ship of theseus)

and your house is too quiet
            shouts and the pitter patter of feet
pounding fill hollowed out floorboards, hallways
gutted inside out jaw open stiff and blue at the
fingers–it mocks you to live in a place of newly
furrowed despair; what is it that makes you
undeserving of what once was, what is it you've
done to ruin it so?
truthfully, to word it with poignancy is doing it
injustice. it's a bellow from the deepest pits of
my chest, in the tips of my fingers to my toe
beds: i want to be loved. i miss my family. there
is nothing to miss, and i know this, of course,
but still i yearn with my whole body for the
chance to love unapologetically and be loved
back.

shout from rooftops and windowsills picked
open; you will find no reprieve. there is no
noah's ark in a house flooded with grief for one
more broken little boy in a body too big in a
house too small

(6:01 pm
the refrigerator buzzes and you wonder why you
cannot seem to ever be happy. maybe you are
just not meant for it)

late july

i wonder if this is how it is to live. for the world
to convulse for you, to feel the slow and stupid
heartbeat of summer against the sleeves of your
skin.

confront the meaningless of life as an
opportunity for something wonderful; a maker
of beauty soil rimmed palms and earth caked
under your nails, World and you one in the
same. sticking your hands in the dirt and running
down grassy fields and find in others the beauty
of relationship and human connection (i love to
throw pebbles across the lake with you and i
would wait forever for you if that's what you
needed the magpies keep me company at your
doorstep and i love you so much and in another
life i'd like if we could share an orange and fold
laundry, peak through morning blinds and
hurriedly shuffle back under covers)

it is enough to be here. look at yourself and say i
want to live until it comes true, drag your hands
through your hair until you feel real and know
that longing is enough.

hrt grounds lives

most all, i yearn for tangibility.
i want to be rooted in reality. i am tired of being
too little too often, too tired of being an
embarrassing and fleeting thought, a weak
attempt at living
it is embarrassing coming to terms with how
incredibly lackluster i am; i cannot even exist
right
   it is not even a fearful ignition that keeps me
scared, it is a burdening weight. have i ever
stopped to consider it is not my transness, but
my inability to be trans that is the problem
(and i am gently reminded of psalms of
welcoming and open arms and faded scriptures
that smell of rosewood and pine where the pages
crease at the edges and the cover is leather and
everything will be okay and i wish i could be
back there, wide-eyed and 8 and unafraid of the
world, unafraid to be.)
sometimes i consider (a fleeting thought) had i
never transitioned how happy my parents would
be. to be a product of a birthright that glimmered
and gleaned and was a thriving example of
everything it meant to be American, ironically
enough. a perfect world where i was the

machinations and bindings of both God and my
home and my Home, where my mothers tongue
is not just my mothers tongue
i wouldn't, i don't think. i think i have enough
spatial awareness to come to terms with the fact
that i could not pretend to be a good girl, (i am
not a girl and i am far along the reins of being
good) though i play with the idea yearningly,
where i trade a life of inner happiness and found
family for the appeasement of my father for
loving embraces and kisses and warm jackets
and i am dully reminded that i will never be able
to have both

ecclesiastic

colored lights filter through stained glass
window panes
 into the church you've built ground up,
 dirt caked under your nails
the earth of His world is a part of you; you take
what little company you can get)
your dedication is a kirk and you pray
and pray and
pray and
it seems to be all you know how to do—begging
on
your knees to a God that teaches you what it
means to be
pure and all the reasons you are not for
something more.
He will teach you what it means to be guilty;
will
teach you to gut yourself from inside out under
a claim of sanctity

repetition creates faux urgency (a conversation of run ons from and for orestes)

i love you said more as a last resort professing
vulnerability, a poorly masked regard of i don't
want you to die
i love you and i want to spend my life with you
but it's so hard when all i can feel is blood under
my fingers and the spit in my mouth and to be
conscious is too much — is it too much of a
grievance to ask someone to rip my skin inside
out?
how can you recognize me and it is a silly
question, for you have tasted how i am and my
flavor matches your tongue and with flagrancy
you say i was born knowing you
i am so tired & i am sorry & i love you too

the holly and the thematic justice of the world

and listen close;
        to the machinery's buzz (the
machinations of Man and it's coming of—
to play God is a task suited only for those made
in his image and we
 have long relinquished such right as our own)
and the distant calls of a songbird and a world's
gentle hum
        ivy furrows itself into the cracks of a
wall,
buttercups blossom from the shadows of
cemented tiles with initials sloppily scratched
into
the pavement's surface & everything sings and
suddenly it comes to you
rooted deep into our instinctual palette is a
careful,
quiet sort of notion of coexistence with
everything we have ever been,
everything we have ever seen. sinking cities
with communion baked into its boroughs &
        brick veiled in walls of morning glories
unfurling its limbs;

survival and love is one in the same and it is all
we have ever known &
        mortality is a treasure and curse in one
vein &
you are the universe tasting itself, entangled
within a teetering thread of what it is to live
you want to be dandelion fields, alliums that
prick grassy plains,
patches of baby's breath and forget-me-nots and
onslaughts of
orchids. sunrises and rose hips that color trees
brown and bare,
wisteria and all its roots encompass;
        the World and you one in the same. for
all that is Holy, Lord,
please let me stay forever golden

the harp in samuels & the floral chord progression

you spend lazy afternoons in the garden
furrow your brows, knees to chest rocking as
you sing the world sweet wishes and tales of the
Holy.
cupped hands and overgrown cuticles are your
contributions to His symphony; fanciful
ornaments which you swear make all the
difference and when you see how the garden's
sprouts stand a little taller you feel your
suspicions proven right
by God, you are one of his faithful creations
made from and for his bidding

ease found in love, life, & apple orchards

my memory is spotty at times. there are
sometimes weeks, years, even, of my life i don't
remember, moments where months are a matter
of a million gray days folding in on themselves,
forming a thin sleeve against the bridge of my
nose, the tips of my nail beds where all i can
make out is the rushing of blood through my
fingers and the edges of stilted rolls of film
i've been hit with a startling amount of clarity as
of late, though. i think it's a refreshing sort of
realization, a willingness to not be put back into
a cycle of sorts? it's a kind and gentle sort of
thought, kindling crackling in the edge of your
pocket's lining — the world is a beautiful place,
and i don't want to die. the world is a beautiful
place and i am scared to live
a few days past, i stumble across an apple
orchard. it is december and frost covers the
fields all around, or almost all around, reaching
around everywhere but under the apple trees.
rows and rows of shrubbery gathered along the
hilltop and i take an apple. it is sweet and crisp
and i am happy to be there, winter air pricking at
my cheeks and apple juice on my hands.

sometimes i think that's what it means to live. i
woke up the day after trying to kill myself, and i
woke up the day after that and the world is a
beautiful place and i am glad i am alive.

dancing in domesticity

there are worlds where we are invisible, left for
dead—but here, bodies furrowed under
blankets in the presence of a heater's gentle buzz
your arms are wrapped around me and hands
interlocked this sort of intimacy is a gently
glaring
reminder tapping on your window frame of
consciousness that shouts in bright lights and
ceiling tops that You Are Real and You are
Okay.
 the world is a beautiful place and i am glad to
be in
it with you, glad to dance over powdered kitchen
tiles bowls scattered across counter tops & i am
glad you exist.

central guangzhou factory, intertwined with heart

my family moved out of our small house tucked away in a factory's heart in 2006. back then, there was a 1st grader who made paper snowflakes with me and in his place now is a boy hardened by time. in (what is now) their house remains heights etched into walls, doodles on sliding doors— i will lovingly linger in your life, how can you reject me when i am a part of you?

suicidal ideation on a deital level

you love / self sacrificing and all / a weak cry
from your Father's love / blood drawn from
hand to hand /
to die in the warm embrace of plywood plank /
palms pooling red is a mercy you wish onto
yours own / you want to be a thing of threes / a
gentle thing a haunting reminder / love & learn
to be confused in its absence, never despaired /
for him, you would end it all / though that's
never truly been the highest bar of yours to reach
/ for him you feel your Father's grace / taste into
yourself from pits of your stomach / adorations
honey thick / sticky with the hearths of your
very being / ancestral tidings bare bright and
high at the bridge of your nose / finally a
prophet you think yourself / you may finally rest

international voyage

there is an introspective sort of feeling about
recovery
i know healing is not linear, i am well aware of
my toils and the upbringings and causes of such
but i toss and turn and all that comes to mind is a
quiet request. i don't want to hurt this badly all
over again.
it is hard, i tell (to anyone who will listen, really)
when your existence is a burden and a blessing
all in it's own—who am i meant to go to for
support when your birthright is a plaque of
suffrage?
i am sorry for all i have inflicted, for the
hardship you've gone through for me, i profess.
please forgive me.

令和

what do you think about it clamors for your
attention
it is untimely and discordant and i am bitter and
lying because a new start for the body is
commendable and my heart is stuck in the same
place it's always been , the same child i've
always —afraid of the world, himself — you
make me the person i want to be and you are
leaving in place for order

a simple itinerary of what is loved

you love, in a very particular order:
1. those around you
2. what's around you
3. miscellaneous uncategorized
no complicated metaphor of love or yearning or
anything along those lines, is it not simply
enough to feel?
you are far along from times where all you wrote
of was wounds cauterized past any semblance of
vulnerability or mortal longings to not be. you
think that is something to be proud of,
something worth living

太阳

i am sick of waiting to be better.
sick of nights where i etch crooked loneliness
and inner dilemma, of nights where i feel as if i
will never make it past the age of 16. i am sick
of being a tragedy.

there is a certain sick and stupid yearning that
comes with sadness in literature— love is
unobtainable, almost chimerical, but beauty is in
the eye of the beholder and it surrounds you.

to be raw and paradoxical is to be human; how
sweet is it to be wild and free? life is good
because you are here and you are speckled light
that cracks between the seams, the universe
living and breathing it's own code and looking
back at itself, and you are love and i love you.

closing to an empty theater from a tired author / stilted mountainside

& listen close to the low hum and warbling of
cicadas & songbirds' chirps & they come in
couplets & we are constantly splitting bread to
one another & the west wind calls your name &
it says what i dare not & the world loves you &
you were
born to die but there is beauty in death &
calloused hands & the squeaking of a rusted
door hinge & you spend so much of your life
trying to make yourself palatable & do you
remember what you were meant to taste like &
living for the hope of it all is what it means to
live & the body heals itself over
and over again & you will rebuild in spite of it
all & there is somebody who's been trying to
save you all along and it's been you.

sticky backs and the glow pt 2

there will never be another summer like this
again; a wretched poignancy surrounds that fact
and a newly formed hope surrounds us because
maybe it is enough to just be happy in and with
each other. i believe in love because i am full of
it, and i know there is love because you exist.
i figured out why the classic coming of age is so
ingrained in media, art, the world— not
necessarily free of burden but an ideal world,
you'd put your happiness front and foremost. let
yourself be surrounded by those we care about
and care for them back without requisite in light
polluted suburbs and bottom bunk beds.
i need my friends and group hugs and hushed
laughter and furrowed away buildings and love,
tucked and pressed deep in a hearts chamber

www.ingramcontent.com/pod-product-compliance
Lightning Source LLC
LaVergne TN
LVHW050304200726
843509LV00015B/3156